THE LATER YEARS OF
BRITISH RAIL
1980–1995
FREIGHT SPECIAL

PATRICK BENNETT & PETER LOVELL

AMBERLEY

First published 2021

Amberley Publishing
The Hill, Stroud
Gloucestershire, GL5 4EP

www.amberley-books.com

Copyright © Patrick Bennett & Peter Lovell, 2021

The right of Patrick Bennett & Peter Lovell to
be identified as the Authors of this work has
been asserted in accordance with the Copyrights,
Designs and Patents Act 1988.

ISBN 978 1 3981 0293 4 (print)
ISBN 978 1 3981 0294 1 (ebook)

British Library Cataloguing in Publication Data.
A catalogue record for this book is available from
the British Library.

Typesetting by SJmagic DESIGN SERVICES, India.
Printed in the UK.

Contents

Introduction

During the period covered by this book the freight business of British Railways went through changes as great as any that had occurred since the railways began. In 1980 BR was effectively one corporate railway. Freight yards were still busy dealing with mixed trains. Four-wheeled, unbraked or vacuum-braked wagons were the norm. There were still hundreds of collieries supplying an endless stream of trains to power stations. Newspapers, parcels and mail were predominantly carried by rail. Travelling post offices still plied the length and breadth of Britain. As for motive power, most of the modernisation plan locomotives were still in use, although some new types were slowly being introduced.

The first major change came about in 1983 with the formation of a separate freight sector. This was symbolised by the adoption of a new livery for freight sector locomotives. Concurrent with these changes were others less favourable to the freight business: collieries were being closed, general freight was haemorrhaging to road transport and traditional traffics, such as newspapers and mail, started to move to other modes of transport.

In 1987 further change came with the sub-division of the freight business. The new sub-sectors were Coal, Petroleum, Construction, Metals, Railfreight Distribution, Railfreight General and Rail Express Systems. These changes were accompanied by new liveries. The civil engineering sector also had its own dedicated locomotives and livery. By this time vacuum-braked wagons were rapidly disappearing and new more powerful and efficient locomotives had been introduced.

The Conservative government elected in 1992 announced its intention to privatise the railway industry. With this in mind, in 1994 three separate freight businesses were created. These were Loadhaul, Mainline and Transrail. The idea behind this was for the companies to compete with each other for business. In truth the real competition was with road transport and when it came to full privatisation the three companies were purchased as one, and a new company – English, Welsh & Scottish Railways – was created. The Freightliner business was privatised separately.

In this book the authors have set out to portray these great changes as comprehensively as possible, and in doing so create a historical record of a momentous period in the history of the transport of freight by rail. To this end, images from throughout Britain, covering both the small branch lines as well as the major freight arteries, are included. The complete range of traffics from all the freight sectors are shown, as well as every type of motive power active during that period.

The Corporate Railway

Devon and Cornwall

By the late 1970s the only remaining milk traffic was from the West Country and West Wales to London. The 16:42 St Erth–Clapham Junction is seen passing through Liskeard on 2 May 1978 hauled by Class 50 No. 50028 with a mix of 2,000- and 3,000-gallon-capacity tank wagons. After leaving St Erth it would have picked up at Lostwithiel, and will call at Totnes and Exeter St Davids, where traffic from Torrington and Chard Junction would be added. Milk traffic ceased in 1982 when the remaining traffic was transferred to road.

Class 25 No. 25058 passes Tywardreath between Lostwithiel and Par on 26 April 1979 with empty UCV 'clay hood' wagons returning from Fowey Docks to St Blazey. Class 25s were first allocated to Laira (Plymouth) in 1971 where they replaced the Class 22 diesel hydraulics and the Class 42/43 'Warships' on some of their easier turns. They operated mainly from Exeter on local freight and passenger services to Barnstaple and Paignton, and from St Blazey on Cornish freight. From the late 1970s Class 37s in Cornwall, and Class 31s in Devon, replaced them.

Following the closure of the former LSWR north Cornwall line in the 1960s, freight traffic continued to Wadebridge and the Wenford Bridge branch via the former GWR line from Bodmin Road (now Parkway) to Boscarne Junction. On 8 May 1979, Class 08 No. 08643 is seen heading away from Bodmin General on the St Blazey–Wenford Bridge trip. At Boscarne Junction the locomotive will run around before heading up to the clay drys at Wenford Bridge. The Wenford Bridge branch closed in 1983.

On 18 June 1979, Class 31 No. 31284 pulls out of Exeter Riverside Yard with the 08:55 to Walton Old Yard, Warrington. This is a typical mixed vacuum-braked train of the period complete with guards' van. Half the train consists of bitumen tanks that have probably visited Exeter City Basin and are now returning to the Elsemere Port area. The locomotive now faces a 20-mile climb to Whiteball Summit. Although booked for a Type 4 locomotive, this service came low down in the pecking order and was invariably a Class 25 or 31.

Introduced in September 1977, the Speedlink network modernised wagonload services, replacing short wheel base vacuum-braked wagons with modern air-braked vehicles capable of operating at higher speeds. During the early 1980s there was a period of 'dual running' in the West Country, with both vacuum- and air-braked services operating. On 3 September 1981, Class 47 No. 47033 passes Matford, on the outskirts of Exeter, with six vacuum-braked wagons for Plymouth Friary. In the evening a northbound vacuum-braked service would run to Barry, followed by an air-braked service from St Blazey to Severn Tunnel Junction.

Woodhead and Guide Bridge

Construction of the Woodhead line was begun in 1841 by the Sheffield, Ashton-under-Lyne and Manchester Railway. Manchester–Woodhead was completed in 1844, and Sheffield–Dunford Bridge in July 1845. The 3-mile, 22-yard Woodhead Tunnel was completed in December that year. A second bore was completed in 1852. In 1936 the LNER started work on electrifying the line at 1,500 Vdc. Work stopped at the outbreak of the Second World War. In 1948 a new tunnel was started and was completed in 1954. Passenger services ceased in 1970 and the line was closed completely in July 1981. Two types of locomotive were designed by the LNER to work the line, although all but one were actually built by BR. These were the 2,490 hp Co-Co EM2 (later Class 77) and the 1,868 hp Bo+Bo EM1 (later Class 76). From Sheffield to Dunford Bridge, a distance of nearly 20 miles, the line rises continuously at gradients of up to 1 in 100. On 27 May 1980, on the slightly easier 1 in 124 at Hazlehead, we see Class 76 No. 76021 and an unidentified classmate heading a mixed westbound freight.

Most trains on the Woodhead route were double-headed, but in this instance on 27 May 1980 we see a lone Class 76, No. 76040, passing through Huddersfield Junction with a westbound train of coal in 14-ton mineral wagons – still a common sight in 1980. The signal box was abolished in 1998.

Above: Heading through the closed Dunford Bridge station and about to enter Woodhead Tunnel on 18 April 1981 are Class 76 Nos 76006 and 76010 also with coal wagons. Dunford Bridge closed on 5 January 1970 when passenger services on the line were withdrawn.

Right: In the last year of operation, shortly before closure, a merry-go-round coal train from Fiddlers Ferry Power Station passes through the closed Woodhead station hauled by a pair of Class 76s. The first Woodhead station opened in 1844 and was replaced by the one seen here in 1953. Serving a tiny community, remote from the station, it was no surprise that this closed as early as 1964.

Guide Bridge station came into being with the opening of the Sheffield, Ashton and Manchester Railway's Manchester–Sheffield line, at that time open only as far as Godley Toll Bar. Originally named Ashton and Hooley Hill, it became plain Ashton in February 1842, and Guide Bridge in July 1845. It became a junction with the opening of the SA&M line to Stalybridge, and the Manchester and Birmingham line from Stockport – both in the mid-1840s. The picture was completed with the opening of the Oldham Ashton and Guide Bridge Junction line in 1861. It was here at Guide Bridge that diesel traction replaced electric on the Woodhead trains. Towards the end of their career the Class 40s became concentrated in the North West and were a common site around Manchester. In 1981 an unidentified Class 40 heads towards the station with a long rake of coal wagons

Double-headed Class 40 workings were unusual, as we see another long train heading west on the same day. Two other Class 40s await their duties and on the extreme right are parked some of the Class 76 locos.

West London

In the early 1980s the electrified North London line operated a 20-minute passenger service between Richmond and Broad Street (adjacent to Liverpool Street). It also connected Stratford and the North Thames with the other main lines into London. The busiest location was at Acton Wells Junction where the lines from Willesden and Cricklewood joined and there was a short spur down to the Great Western Main Line and Acton Yard. An hour here could often produce a dozen freight trains. On 8 April 1981 the 05:30 Toton East Yard–Acton, headed by Class 25 No. 25176, has joined the North London line from Cricklewood at the junction opposite the signal box. After a short distance it has now taken the spur to descend down to Acton Yard. The line on the right continues down to Kew Junction and Richmond.

The Class 50s were transferred from the London Midland Region to the Western Region from 1974 following electrification of the West Coast Main Line between Crewe and Glasgow. They were rarely used on freight duties, but on 12 April 1981 No. 50043 has just passed under the North London line and is approaching Acton Main Line with the 13:12 Norwood Junction–Acton Yard working composed mainly of 16-ton MCV mineral wagons. The locomotive had probably worked up to Paddington on one of the Thames Valley commuter services in the morning and was now being used on a fill-in turn before returning to passenger duty in the evening.

Willesden South Western Sidings linked the North London line with the West Coast Main Line yards at Wembley and the West London line to Kensington Olympia and Clapham Junction. On 6 July 1981, Class 25 Nos 25311 and 25266 are seen reversing out of the sidings with a mix of Freightliner and Speedlink VAA vans. The electrified tracks on the left are the North London lines. The tracks from South Western Sidings ran parallel with the North London line as far as Acton Wells Junction where they first joined the Midland line from Cricklewood and then the North London line. It was not uncommon for trains from Cricklewood to arrive at Acton Wells Junction and then reverse back into Willesden South Western Sidings.

The Tyne Yard–Ridham Dock (Sittingbourne) coal trains were the longest working on BR with HAA MGR (merry-go-round) wagons. In the early 1980s locomotives were changed at Cricklewood Yard. For the final lap to Ridham Dock the Southern Region would provide either a pair of pair of Class 33 diesels or often a pair of Class 73 electro-diesels. Between Cricklewood and Kew Junction, with no third rail, the Class 73s would need to rely on their 600-bhp diesel engines. On 7 July 1981, Class 73 Nos 73106 and 73125 are seen crawling up the incline between Neasden Junction and Acton Canal Wharf with the 22:05 Tyne Yard–Ridham Dock. Once they have reached Acton Wells it will be downhill to Kew Junction and the electrified third rail.

The Peak District

Buxton Lime Firms resulted from the amalgamation in 1891 of a number of limestone quarries in the Peak District. In 1926, BLF became wholly owned by ICI, its main customer. The quarries are now operated by Tarmac. On 28 September 1981, Class 25 No. 25081 emerges from Dove Holes Quarry with a long rake of limestone wagons. These wagons were actually iron ore tippler wagons, originally introduced for the domestic iron ore quarrying industry. The building on the right has since been demolished.

The 1980s would see up to a dozen trains a day making the journey from the quarries at Tunstead to the ICI works at Winnington. The majority were hauled by Class 25s, as seen here. A load of 1,200 tons might seem excessive for a Type 2 locomotive, but the Class 25s were sturdy little engines and at the start of their journey up this 1 in 90 gradient they were always banked. Class 25 No. 25106 is seen on 12 October 1981.

An unusual working at Peak Forest as we see Class 45 'Peak' No. 45003 with another load of limestone for ICI. Despite its 2,500 hp it still requires a banker – in this case in the shape of a Class 40. These vacuum-braked bogie hopper wagons were purchased by ICI in 1936 and were in use until December 1997 when they were replaced by more modern rolling stock.

Chinley station still has its four platforms despite having lost two of the tracks through the station just the year before. The junction between the Midland Railway's Peak Forest and Hope Valley lines was just to the east of Chinley, making this at one time a very busy route. In 1982 Class 40 No. 40079 trundles down the 1 in 90 with yet another train of limestone for ICI Winnington.

At the other end of the route there is a stiff climb after Northwich station before Class 25 No. 25249 will be able to turn off the main line onto the Winnington Branch. The photograph dates from 14 May 1981.

Another important traffic emanating from the Peak District is cement from the Hope Cement Works. The works is connected to the Hope Valley main line by a 2-mile-long branch. This leads into the exchange sidings controlled from Earles Sidings' signal box. On 21 May 1981, Class 40 No. 40139 pulls out of the sidings with a long rake of Presflo tanks.

Mail

On 6 September 1980, Class 40 No. 40024 emerges from Welwyn North Tunnel with a parcels train, for which happily it is displaying the correct headcode discs. In those days it would be unthinkable for the railways not to be the prime movers of mail, parcels and newspaper trains – a vast change to the present day. No. 40024 spent most of its career in the North West. In 1962 it was named *Lucania*. It was withdrawn from Longsight in 1984.

On 1 June 1980, Class 31 No. 31222 stands at Peterborough with a mail train destined for Kings Cross. The Class 31s were originally fitted with the Mirrlees, Bickerton and Day JSV12 engine. The early machines in the series were rated at 1,250 hp, later ones at 1,350 hp and others at 1,600 hp. One was even rated at 2,000 hp. However, this was not a successful engine and between 1965 and 1969 the whole class was re-engined with the English Electric 12SVT, rated at 1,470 hp.

By the early 1980s there was just one diesel locomotive on BR left in original green livery: No. 40106. Following its entry into works for overhaul and repaint, there was much surprise to see it re-emerging back in green, as seen here at Guide Bridge in 1981, heading towards Manchester with a long parcels train.

The Aberdeen portion of the Up West Coast Postal heads through Errol on 11 July 1980 hauled by Class 26 No. 26037. Leaving Aberdeen at around 15:30, this would join up with the larger Glasgow portion further south before continuing to London. Errol was a small wayside station between Dundee and Perth. The platforms were so low that steps were provided – hopefully they would be in the right place if you were disembarking.

Coal

In the early 1980s there was still a significant amount of coal traffic conveyed in 21-ton HTV wagons between Severn Tunnel Junction and Acton Yard, where trains would be split up and tripped to their final destination. Class 47s were the normal traction, but on 13 February 1981 Class 46 No. 46032 makes an unusual appearance in the London area, as it heads west through Iver on the GW Main Line with empties for South Wales. Behind the locomotive are more HTV wagons stored in the loop, probably awaiting scrap or conversion to engineers' wagons.

Just north of Royston, Class 56 No. 56074 passes south with a train of MGR empties, probably heading for Grimethorpe colliery. Note that at the date of this photograph, 18 April 1981, this was still a four-track railway; in fact, until 1968 this was the main route between Sheffield and Leeds. In 1968, due to subsidence, passenger traffic was switched to the Swinton and Knottingley line but reverted to this line in 1972. In the early 1980s it switched back once more to the Swinton and Knottingley line and in 1988 the line was closed to through traffic. Today there is just a single track serving the glass factory at Monk Bretton. In the early 1980s No. 56074 and two other machines were fitted with an orange flashing light, as seen here. This was for use when the trains were under automatic control unloading coal. The experiment was not continued with.

On 27 October 1981, Class 47 No. 47242 passes through Chester with a rake of MGR coal wagons from Point of Ayr Colliery destined for Fiddlers Ferry Power Station. Point of Ayr Colliery closed in 1996.

It was the North Midland Railway that completed the line from Derby to Chesterfield, with the line opening in July 1840. On 10 May 1844 the NMR, the MCR and the Birmingham and Derby Junction Railway merged to form the Midland Railway. Near Tapton Junction, just north of Chesterfield, on 18 September 1981, Class 40 No. 40082 with a train of 21-ton coal hoppers, switches from the Down Main to the Down Goods in order to proceed towards Barrow Hill.

Other Traffic

The Class 45 and similar Class 46 'Peaks' were primarily express passenger locomotives. The introduction of the Class 45s transformed services on the Midland Main Line. They were also to be found on trans-Pennine and cross country services. Freight working was less usual until later in their careers. In 1981, Class 45 No. 45110 heads south through Sheffield with a train of Cemflo tanks. No. 45110 has been adorned with the unofficial name of *Medusa* by the staff at Tinsley depot.

By 1980 Class 37s were replacing Class 27s on the West Highland line. On 19 June 1980 a Speedlink service departs from Garelochead behind Class 37 No. 37027. The first two wagons are from the VAA/VBA/VCA family of long wheelbase four-wheeled wagons that replaced the old short wheelbase vacuum-braked Vanfits, allowing increased speed with a much greater payload.

On 30 August 1980, Class 37 No. 37171, having previously loaded at the sand quarry at Middleton Towers, waits in the yard at Kings Lynn ready to depart for Monk Bretton.

In the summer of 1980, Class 25 No. 25103 blasts up the 1 in 100 gradient on the line out of Chester towards Warrington with a train of Dogfish ballast wagons. No. 25103 only had a few more weeks left in service, being withdrawn on 7 September the same year.

Oil/Tanks

At one time the Stanlow Refinery in Cheshire made considerable use of rail transport for its products. This is no longer the case. The exchange sidings have been removed and movement is now mostly by pipeline. Nearly forty years ago, on 2 September 1981, Class 25 No. 25251 accelerates away from Helsby Junction with a train from Stanlow consisting mostly of TTA gas oil wagons with one TCA LPG bogie wagon.

The North and West line from Shrewsbury to Newport lost its express passenger services in the late 1960s when they were re-routed via Birmingham. In the 1980s it maintained a healthy level of freight traffic between Scotland, the North West and Wales and the West Country. On 8 May 1981, Class 47 No. 47332 is seen entering Hereford with bogie oil tankers that have probably originated from the Ellesmere Port area. The train is taking one of the loops around the back of the station so will be changing crews or stabling for the weekend.

Freightliner

At Ipswich on 21 August 1980 Class 47 No. 47162 passes through the station with a train of containers from Felixstowe. No. 47162 was a Stratford engine, the clue being the white painted roof, a feature for which Stratford engines were renowned. Notice the mixture of colour light and semaphore signals. The IG on the signal post indicates that these signals were controlled by Ipswich Goods Junction signal box, which can just be seen in the background.

The signalman at Auchterarder has wasted no time in returning the home signal to danger as Class 47 No. 47207 climbs towards Gleneagles with a southbound Freightliner intermodal train on 10 July 1980. The containers all carry Freightliner's red and grey branding. When first established Freightliner was intended for the UK domestic market using its own containers, but growth came from maritime traffic through UK ports conveying containers owned by the shipping companies.

The Railfreight Sector is Created

Devon and Cornwall

The Speedlink Network operated by running trunk services between two dozen marshalling yards and secondary distribution sites to a fixed timetable. This provided a faster and more reliable service than conventional wagonload freight. By 1984 Speedlink was running 150 trunk services daily, serving a potential 800 destinations. On 2 August 1984, Class 31 No. 31286 passes Cockwood Harbour with a short trip freight from Heathfield to Exeter Riverside, where it will be attached to a St Blazey–Severn Tunnel Junction bulk service.

Until the late 1970s the Barnstaple line carried a healthy amount of freight. The loss of the Torrington milk traffic in 1978 and the clay traffic from Meeth in 1982 removed the two main flows. By 1984 cement was the main traffic and on 25 September 1984 Class 31 No. 31294 is seen at Cowley Bridge Junction with the 08:55 Barnstaple–Exeter Riverside comprising four PCA cement wagons. Freight facilities were finally withdrawn from Barnstaple in 1987, although Lapford remained open to traffic (mainly fertiliser) until 1991.

The bulk of Cornwall's china clay production was exported through Fowey Docks and there was a constant stream of trains from the clay drys in the St Austell and Par areas to Lostwithiel, where trains reversed to access the Fowey branch. On 26 June 1987 Class 37 No. 37196 pulls into the down loop at Lostwithiel with empty wagons from Fowey. On the right-hand side refurbished Class 37/6 No. 37674 waits to depart with a loaded train. Both locomotives are in Railfreight large logo grey livery with red solebar.

South Wales

The Cardiff Canton Class 56s were used on a range of duties including oil trains and an evening freightliner from Pengam as far as Crewe. They were also used in pairs on the Port Talbot Docks–Llanwern iron ore trains. These had previously been triple-headed by Class 37s. On 3 April 1984, Nos 56050 and 56052 are nearing their journey's end as they pass through Newport with a loaded train.

Despite the introduction of air-braked wagons, vacuum-braked wagons continued to operate in South Wales until the early 1990s. The 23 April 1987 was not a good day to be hanging washing beside the line at Marshfield as Class 37 No. 37258 leaves a cloud of coal dust as it heads towards Newport Docks with a long rake of MDV wagons from Maesteg. At Newport local and imported coal was blended, most of it then being used at nearby Uskmouth Power Station.

Railfreight had been established in 1982 as a separate division of British Rail responsible for all freight operations. Initially there was little visible change, but after a while locomotives began to appear in the new Railfeight grey livery with large logo. On 23 April 1987 Class 47 No. 47112 is seen passing through Severn Tunnel Junction with a westbound oil tank train. On the adjacent line is a Class 37 waiting to enter the marshalling yard.

Severn Tunnel Junction was the major marshalling yard for South Wales and a key interchange point for sorting traffic between South Wales and the rest of the UK. On the evening of 23 April 1987, Class 37 No. 37255 departs westwards with HAA wagons. It has recently been repainted in the new Railfreight livery with red solebar. With the decline in coal and industrial production and increasing fixed-train formations, the marshalling yard and locomotive depot were closed on 12 October 1987.

At Gaer Junction the lines from the western valleys (that served Ebbw Vale and a number of collieries) joined the South Wales Main Line for traffic heading east. Traffic for Newport Docks and westbound destinations would join at Ebbw Junction a mile further west. On 28 May 1987, Class 37 No. 37159 cautiously joins the main line with a train of mixed ballast wagons from the quarry at Machen.

The South (Hampshire, Wiltshire and Oxfordshire)

Most of the container services to Southampton during this period were hauled by Class 47s, but a pair of Class 33s were normally provided for the morning return trip to Willesden. On 19 April 1984, Class 33 Nos 33117 and 33021 are seen passing under Battledown Flyover with the 11:15 Willesden–Millbrook. They are taking the Salisbury line rather than the direct route to Southampton and Bournemouth. In 1983 the eastern side of the triangle at Salisbury Tunnel Junction had been reinstated, enabling traffic direct access to Southampton via Winchester or Andover.

China clay had traditionally passed through Fowey Docks for export. The introduction of modern air-braked wagons provided greater opportunities and a flow was established between St Blazey and Biberest in Switzerland using the train ferry from Dover. Class 47 No. 47304 is seen approaching Crofton on the Berks & Hants line with the 06:15 St Blazey–Dover on 27 March 1986. On occasions the load would be heavier and tripped to Exeter in two portions before proceeding to Dover.

Class 33/1 No. 33118 approaches Southampton Central with a train of continuous welded rails from Redbridge Permanent Way depot on 31 October 1986. The Class 33/1 sub-class were designed to operate TC units in push-pull mode between Bournemouth and Weymouth before this section was electrified. Only three were required to operate the scheduled service and the remainder of the class could be found on passenger and freight duties.

There was little freight traffic west of Southampton, but a regular flow was oil from the Wytch Farm estate at Furzebrook near Poole to the Esso refinery at Fawley. On 31 July 1987, Class 47 No. 47521 is heading through Bournemouth with empty bogie tank wagons from Fawley to Furzebrook. Shortly afterwards production at Wytch Farm was increased and a pipeline built to Fawley and Hamble.

In the late 1970s BR determined a need for more Type 5 freight locomotives to handle projected freight growth. The Class 56s were being problematic to put into service, and a design that was cheaper to produce and maintain, and had export potential, was specified. The Class 58s were an innovative modular design with all of the key components (cabs, power unit, radiator, turbocharger and electrical equipment) fitted as easily interchangeable modules on the load-bearing underframe. Entering service in 1983, the Class 58s were initially employed on coal trains from the Nottingham coalfield. On 6 August 1987, No. 58009 is seen south of Culham, approaching Didcot with an MGR service for the Power Station.

The Midlands

Bayston Hill Quarry, just south of Shrewsbury, was a major supplier of railway ballast for the North West. On 11 May 1984, Class 47 No. 47327 takes the middle road through Shrewsbury, with the 10:20 Bayston Hill–Guide Bridge comprising seven 40-ton hoppers.

Near Tapton Junction, just north of Chesterfield in the summer of 1987, a pair Class 20s, newly outshopped in green livery, with No. 20064 leading, switch from the Down main to the Down Goods in order to proceed towards Barrow Hill with their train of steel empties.

Parcels

Class 47 No. 47538 has just passed Marazion on 24 June 1985 with the 19:22 Penzance–Paddington TPO. At this stage the train still travelled with sorting staff for the whole journey. With the introduction of postcodes and automated sorting, on board sorting quickly declined. Soon all of the Cornish mail would be taken to Plymouth, sorted and returned for delivery on the westbound service.

On a number of weekends during the winter of 1985/86 the West of England Main Line between Exeter and Taunton was closed with diversions via Yeovil Junction and Honiton. This bought the rare sight of a parcels train on the former LSWR main line. As the sun sets on 7 December 1985, Class 47 No. 47205 passes through the closed Seaton Junction station with the 13:50 Plymouth–Leeds parcels.

In the 1980s all of the major London termini operated a range of newspaper, mail and parcels trains that left in the small hours. These would often return empty to London. On 11 March 1987, Class 33/1 No. 33118 has arrived at Clapham Junction, with the 07:28 ECS from Bournemouth consisting of a selection of TPO, BGs and GUVs. This area of traffic declined with the loss of newspaper traffic in July 1987.

London and the Home Counties

In the early 1980s the former GW/GC Joint Line from London through High Wycombe to Aylesbury and Banbury was part of the London Midland Region. Household rubbish was carried in containers from Northolt to the landfill site at Calvert north of Aylesbury. Cricklewood depot provided locomotives, although the wagons were maintained at Old Oak Common. On 21 November 1984, Class 45/1 No. 45137 is coming off the Greenford loop at West Ealing with a short rake of container flats for Old Oak Common.

By 1984 all 135 Class 56s had been delivered and the Western Region had twenty-eight split between Cardiff Canton and Bristol Bath Road. The latter were generally used on stone traffic from the Westbury area where they were often used in pairs, despite being the most powerful freight locomotives on BR. On 7 December 1984, Nos 56035 and 56046 are heading through West Ealing with the 10:20 Purfleet–Merehead stone empties.

During the mid-1980s Foster Yeoman were becoming increasingly dissatisfied with the performance and availability of BR locomotives, particularly the new Class 56s. They already provided their own wagons and negotiated with BR to buy their own locomotives. Tenders were sought from suppliers for locomotives offering 95 per cent availability and four Class 59s were ordered from EMD, part of General Motors. Features included wheel-creep control, which eliminated the need for double-heading because of its superior traction. The locomotives were delivered from Illinois to Southampton on 21 January 1986. On 20 February 1986, No. 59004 is seen climbing the spur to Acton Wells Junction with the 09:28 Acton Yard–Purfleet.

Stratford has been transformed beyond all recognition since the arrival of the DLR and renovation for the London Olympics in 2012. Virtually all freight took the Channelsea Curve to the North London line or Temple Mills Yard. The only exception was the Marks Tey–Mile End sand train. On a dull 12 May 1986, Class 37 No. 37086 double-heads Class 31 No. 31212 through Stratford with the returning empties from Mile End.

On 19 September 1986, Class 85 No. 85006 ambles northwards on the West Coast Main Line at Ledburn Junction with a short, mixed, air-braked freight. These workings were normally handled by Class 31 diesels. Slightly south of here on 8 August 1963 the Great Train Robbery took place when the 18:50 Glasgow–Euston TPO was stopped and robbed of £2.6 million of used banknotes.

Household waste from the west of London was compacted and either taken from Northolt to Calvert or Brentford to Appleford for disposal in landfill sites. During the week the Brentford to Appleford train ran overnight, except on Sundays when it ran in the morning. By 1987 it was normally a Class 56, but on Sundays could be anything spare on Old Oak Common. On Sunday 29 March 1987 the duty has been given to Class 47 No. 47621, seen here in pristine InterCity livery approaching Shottesbrooke, between Reading and Maidenhead, with the return service from Appleford.

By the late 1980s Class 31s were very common on the southern part of the West Coast Main Line, having replaced Class 25s on the lighter freights and engineers' trains. A regular turn for a pair of Class 31s was the Pitstone–Kings Cross cement train. On 14 August 1987 Nos 31161 and 31165 are seen heading south at Soulbury with the empty cement tanks. Earlier this train had worked north from Kings Cross to Bletchley where the locomotives had run round to enable them to access the north-facing entrance to the cement works at Pitstone. No. 31161 is in the early Railfreight grey large logo livery.

The first step towards sectorisation of Railfreight took place in November 1986 when the Speedlink Coal Network (SCN) was established for the distribution of household coal and to small industrial users. Bulk trainloads were delivered to hubs at Didcot, Healey Mills, Millerhill, Pantyffynon, Washwood Heath and Radyr. Circuits were operated from each hub delivering coal direct to yards and installations. Generally, HEA wagons were used, hauled by a dedicated fleet of twenty-five Class 37s. On 24 September 1987, Class 37 No. 37127 passes Waltham St Lawrence, between Reading and Maidenhead, with the 11:08 Didcot–Aylesbury – a circuit that could visit Neasden and return via Oxford. It has just been preceded by No. 37251 with three HEA wagons on the 10:20 Didcot–Chessington.

The Era of Full Sectorisation

Scotland

On 26 March 1991 Class 47 No. 47526 waits in the loop at Inverurie with a southbound Speedlink service. At its peak the Speedlink service was carrying 8 million tonnes per annum. It closed down not long after this photograph was taken.

On 1 August 1995 Class 37 Nos 37801 and 37170 blast up the gradient on their way to Killoch Washery with a train from Chalmerston opencast mine.

Class 37 No. 37095 heads away from Carnoustie on the 23 June 1988 with a mixed Speedlink trip working. It is probably destined for Millerhill or Mossend.

The Aberdeen–Euston 'West Coast Postal' left Perth soon after 17:00. Later mail from Scotland was conveyed on the 21:11 Perth–Carlisle, seen here departing from Perth behind celebrity Class 47 No. 47522 on 27 June 1988. In October 1987 it had been repainted in LNER apple green and named *Doncaster Enterprise*.

By the late 1980s the Class 26s had been ousted from their Highland and north of Scotland line duties by Class 37s and 47s. On 27 June 1988, No. 26035 is heading towards Dalwhinnie at Dalnaspidal with a short engineers' train.

There were still plenty of semaphore signals at Stirling as Class 26 No. 26039 passes through with a short Speedlink trip working on a dull 1 July 1988.

Introduced in 1974 for Anglo-Scottish passenger traffic, the Class 87s were very much 'top link' locomotives in 1989 despite the Class 90s coming on stream between 1987 and 1990. It was surprising that they were used in pairs on steel trains from Ravenscraig. On 20 June 1989 Nos 87009 and 87010 are heading south through the Upper Clyde Valley.

The fifty Class 90s were introduced between 1987 and 1990. With a top speed of 110 mph and push-pull fitted it was surprising that within months most were allocated to the Railfreight and Parcels sectors. On 28 May 1991, No. 90048 is heading south at Dinwoodie Mains with the 15:00 Mossend–Tavistock Junction.

From 1987 the Parcels sector adopted Post Office red livery for its rolling stock. The southbound West Coast Postal is seen south of Wamphray on 28 May 1991 headed by Class 86/4 No. 86419. The first vehicle is in blue and grey, and the last two are in InterCity and Network Southeast liveries.

By 1991 the Class 87s were allocated to the InterCity sector and steel trains on the West Coast Main Line were in the hands of Class 37s. On 29 May 1991, Nos 37285 and 37108 head south at Wamphray with a Mossend–Washwood Heath working.

By 1991 the Class 81–85 electrics had virtually all been withdrawn. With only some new Class 91s assigned to the Distribution sector, most freight on the West Coast Main Line in Scotland was diesel hauled. On 30 May 1991, Class 37/5 No. 37511 in Metal sector livery crosses the Clyde at Crawford with a southbound steel train.

Class 47 No. 47605 had been fitted with ETH (electric train heating) in 1984. With declining passenger work it was allocated to Railfreight in 1988 and subsequently to the Speedlink sector based at Tinsley. On 30 May 1991 it is approaching Crawford with a northbound Speedlink service.

The North East

On 27 February 1993, Class 56 No. 56102 passes Ferrybridge signal box with an MGR train. In the background is the vast bulk of Ferrybridge B Power Station, closed the previous year and subsequently demolished. The signal box has been closed and replaced by a new signalling centre on the other side of the tracks, also named Ferrybridge.

Drax Power Station, with its 3,960-megawatt capacity, consumed up to 36,000 tonnes of coal per day. On 5 September 1992, No. 56095 leaves with empties as another train arrives to discharge its load in the background. These days the majority of trains bring biomass.

The route via Diggle was not the first railway through the Pennines. The route via the Calder Valley opened in 1841. The section of this route between Milner Royd Junction and Bradley Junction lost its passenger service in 1970 but regained it in 2000 with the opening of Brighouse station. Just west of Brighouse on 25 July 1994, Class 37 No. 37717 heads east with a tank train.

One of the main freight flows on the East Coast Main Line north of Newcastle was Scottish coal for blending in the Aire Valley power stations. On 13 August 1991, Class 56 No. 56095 heads north at Alnmouth with the 15:00 York–Millerhill empties.

The line from Northallerton to Leyburn was constructed by the York, Newcastle and Berwick Railway between 1848 and 1858. Leyburn to Hawes was built by the NER, and Garsdale to Hawes by the Midland Railway. The NER section lost its passenger service in 1954 and the Midland section provided a passenger service until 1959. Freight continued in later years to serve only the quarry at Redmire. Subsequently, the MOD took an interest in the line in order to transport tanks to its Catterick base. In 2000 the Wensleydale Railway plc took out a lease on the line and from 2003 has run passenger services. A number of stations have been reopened. On 29 May 1992, as a loaded train returns from Redmire hauled by Class 60 No. 60031, a member of the crew descends to open the crossing gates at Wensley station. This traffic ceased shortly after the photograph was taken.

This train is from the Melkridge opencast site. At the time the photograph was taken, on 28 August 1991, the signalling at Melkridge had not been fully installed so that trains had to leave westbound to Carlisle, as this train is doing, before running round and heading back east. Denton Village crossing box remains in use. Notice the unusual signal post.

By 1991 most of Tyne Yard was used to store engineers' wagons. On 13 August 1991, Class 37 No. 37221, in Dutch livery, pulls out with a train of ZBA Rudd wagons rebuilt from HDVs.

It is the end of the working day and in February 1990 a Class 31 with an engineering train passes under the signal cabin at Hexham, from where this photograph was taken, on its way back to the depot.

Just east of Newport East Junction on 5 April 1994, Class 60 No. 60052 heads towards Middlesbrough with a train of empty BBA steel wagons destined for the Lackenby Works. In the background is the famous Newport Lift Bridge, which unfortunately no longer lifts.

The North West

The Chester & Birkenhead Railway opened its line in September 1840. It became part of the Birkenhead, Lancashire & Cheshire Junction Railway in 1847. The latter company opened the line from Chester to Warrington in December 1850. In August 1859, the BL&CJ was taken over by the GWR and LNWR to become the Birkenhead Joint, an identity it retained until nationalisation. On 3 June 1991, Class 20 Nos 20154 and 20186 head through Helsby with a train bound for Fiddlers Ferry Power Station. The station master's house, the station buildings and the signal box are all listed structures. The line to the left is to Chester, and that to the right to Stanlow and Hooton.

In 1985 the line between Broadheath and Warrington was closed to all traffic. A short section as far as Latchford Junction was retained to allow trains from Walton Old Junction Yard to reach Fiddlers Ferry Power Station. This was accomplished by means of a reversal on this short section of line. On 24 June 1991, Class 20 Nos 20141 and 20013 haul the train away from Latchford Sidings towards Fiddlers Ferry. The signal box is Arpley Junction.

The line from Warrington to Widnes via Fiddlers Ferry was opened by the St Helens Canal and Railway in 1853. The SHC&R later became part of the LNWR. In 1962, passenger services were withdrawn but the line remained open for freight. From the end of the 1960s the principal traffic was MGR coal trains to Fiddlers Ferry Power Station. Such a train passes Monks Siding signal box on 10 May 1992. The box dates to 1875 and is a listed building.

Near Grange-over-Sands on 6 June 1992, Class 60 No. 60066 runs alongside the Kent estuary with returning coal empties from Padiham Power Station.

On 6 April 1988, Class 37 Nos 37676 and 37686 both in Railfreight red-stripe livery climb the 1 in 87 through New Mills South Junction with a Northwich to Peak Forest train of empty ICI hoppers. In the left background is Newtown Viaduct on the line to Hazel Grove and Northenden.

The Stockport, Disley & Whaley Bridge Railway completed its line to Buxton in 1863. In the same year the Midland Railway reached Buxton from the south. The SD&WB was absorbed by the LNW in 1866. Meanwhile the Midland built a route as far as New Mills, from where it could access Manchester. This was completed in 1867. The LNW line from Ashbourne to Buxton via Hindlow was completed in 1894. The Ashbourne line lost its passenger service in 1954 and closed completely in 1967, except for the short section to Hindlow. The Midland route was closed to both passenger and freight between Matlock and Miller's Dale in 1968, but the line from Buxton to Manchester remained open for freight. The LNW route itself came close to closure in 1964. Buxton has for a long time been an important centre for the quarrying of limestone, all of which travels via the Midland line. This particular train, seen on 14 April 1993, is a Tunstead to Hindlow working, seen between Buxton and Hindlow and hauled by Class 37 No. 37688.

Class 31 No. 31444 heads south with a mail train, just south of Lostock Junction, the signal gantry of which can be seen in the background. The signal box was abolished shortly after this photograph was taken on 20 May 1989. Note that the third and fifth coaches are TPOs, which once had pick-up/drop-off equipment fitted.

A type of train sadly no longer with us is this Bolton–St Pancras parcels train, entering Stockport station headed by Class 47 No. 47543 on 26 June 1991. By this stage the Parcels sector operated with a dedicated fleet of Class 31/4s, 47/4s and some Class 86 electrics.

Heading south at Winwick Junction on 2 May 1995 are Nos 47206 and 92030 with a test train. No. 92030 had worked the train over Shap, and the pair are heading back to Crewe. The Class 92s were introduced for Channel Tunnel traffic. They were dual voltage, so able to operate on 750 Vdc third rail or from 25 kV overhead power supplies, enabling them to work between Calais and Scotland.

In connection with a freight exhibition in 1992 three Class 90s were painted in European liveries. No. 90029 received DB livery, No. 90030 received SNCF livery and No. 90028, as seen here, received Belgian Railways livery. No. 90028 is seen on 2 May 1995 on the WCML north of Warrington with 6M79 the Mossend–Washwood Heath Euro Feeder.

On 21 May 1991, at Acton Bridge, Class 90 No. 90045 heads south with a Freightliner service.

Seen on the same date, Class 85 No. 85110 has only a few months left in service before withdrawal later that year. One of a sub-class of fifteen locomotives modified for freight work, it is seen at Acton Bridge with a Dagenham–Halewood working.

On 3 June 1991, Class 31 No. 31565 is seen on the Up Slow just north of Hartford Junction on the WCML with a short rake of Catfish and Dogfish ballast wagons.

Kingmoor Yard opened in 1963 to replace Carlisle's six pre-grouping yards and numerous transfer trips. By the time it opened traffic was in decline and it never achieved its potential. By 29 June 1989, as Class 85 No. 85028 departs with the 15:00 Coatbridge–Tavistock Junction, most of the sidings had been lifted and the yard was mainly used for stabling and crew changing.

The original line to Widnes station (originally called Runcorn Gap) was the one that can be seen going straight on in the background. This line led to a flat crossing with the line to St Helens. In order to avoid this a new line – the Widnes Deviation – was built from Carterhouse Junction to West Deviation Junction. On this line a new station was built, which eventually became Widnes South. On 27 April 1995, Class 31 No. 31142 is seen with a Ditton Junction–Warrington working. The men standing by the level crossing are waiting to take their cows across to the pasture on the left of the line. The cows will stay there until the autumn. The Carterhouse Junction box was abolished in 2006 and demolished the following year.

Class 31 No. 31319 sets off from the Otis Euro Transrail depot at Ordsall Lane with a working to Guinness Park Royal. The date is 30 June 1995, and it is the penultimate week of operation of this service. Guinness no longer uses rail transport and there is no longer a freight facility at Ordsall Lane.

Above: The Cheshire Midland Railway built the line from Atrincham to Northwich in 1863, while the West Cheshire Railway extended the line to Helsby in1869. These two companies became part of the Cheshire Lines Committee, which was a joint railway owned by the GNR, MS&L and MR. Near Delamere on 2 September 1991, Class 47 No. 47368 heads east with a train of tanks.

Right: On 31 May 1995, Class 56 No. 56046 is seen leaving Glazebrook Exchange Sidings with train 6M67 – empty tanks bound for Lindsey.

This scene is considerably changed as the Liverpool–Manchester line is now electrified. Eccles signal box has survived, due to the need to operate the points leading to the Weaste oil terminal line – the line seen on the left, which passes under the main line and runs alongside the Manchester Ship Canal. On 10 January 1994, No. 60007 hauls a rake of tanks towards the main line.

Under sectorisation nuclear flask traffic was allocated to the coal sector and a handful of Class 31s were based at Workington for Sellafield traffic. On 29 June 1989, No. 31276, in coal sector livery, approaches Carlisle Kingmoor Yard with two flasks.

At Brewery Sidings, on 10 February 1992, Class 60 No. 60080 passes with a southbound 'binliner' train. The signals left to right are: Down Goods, and on the bracket Down Main to Down Goods, and Down Main. The distants were controlled by Thorpes Bridge Junction box. Both boxes were abolished in 1998.

Wales

With the closure of Severn Tunnel Junction Yard and the locomotive depot there was a need to stable locomotives for the Newport Yards at East Usk, Ebbw Junction and Alexandra Dock Junction. A stabling point was opened at Godfrey Road, adjacent to Newport station, and up to fifteen Class 37s and a couple of Class 47s could normally be seen here. On 29 April 1989, Class 47 No. 47333 and a selection of Class 37/0, 37/6 and 37/7s are on display in various liveries.

At Croes Newydd, on 18 May 1991, No. 37138 heads south with an empty steel train. The Up Goods loop and the Watery Road Sidings are seen on the right. The sidings have since disappeared under housing. Coming in from the left is the goods branch from Minera, which has since been lifted.

During the 1980s a lot of Class 37s were refurbished, with some re-engined. The Class 37/7s were rewired, the generator replaced with an alternator and additional ballast added to increase adhesion. They replaced the Class 56s on the Port Talbot–Llanwern iron ore trains. On 29 September 1989, Nos 37717 and 37712 are approaching Marshfield with empties returning from Llanwern to Port Talbot.

On 29 September 1989, Class 37 No. 37264 in large logo livery has arrived at Ebbw Junction with coal in vacuum-braked MDV wagons from one of the collieries in the western valleys. It is reversing back to reach Newport Docks where the coal will be blended. By this time Ebbw Junction Yard was mainly used for engineers' wagons.

On the evening of 20 June 1991, Class 56 No. 56032 heads away from Ebbw Junction Yard, Newport, with empty steel wagons. All of the high-voltage electricity lines are heading towards East Usk Power Station.

With the arrival of the Class 60s there was finally a locomotive that could handle the Port Talbot–Llanwern traffic without double-heading. No. 60034 crosses the River Usk at Newport on 26 November 1991 with a loaded train.

On 26 November 1991, Class 37 No. 37891 joins the South Wales Main Line at Maindee Junction, Newport, with empty Cawoods containers from Elsemere Port. Classified as PFAs the wagons carried 20-foot open containers for coal exports to Northern Ireland. A few were also used on the Speedlink Coal Network.

Class 08 No. 08993 passes the former station of Pontyates with a rake of HEA wagons bound for the Cwmmawr disposal point. This locomotive was one of a class of five, designated 08/9, with specially cut-down cabs to work the line to Cwmmawr. This was necessitated by the low bridges on the line, which had started life as a canal. The Burry Port and Gwendreath Valley Railway started freight operations in 1869, with passenger services following in 1909. The latter lasted only until 1953. The last freight train ran on 29 March 1996. The date of this photograph is 19 February 1992.

At Holywell Junction, on 24 June 1993, Class 37 No. 37509 heads east with an engineers' train. The appearance of quadruple track is given by the Up and Down Goods loops, which at this time were over a mile long. Holywell Junction signal box was abolished in 2018 and the line is now controlled from the Wales Rail Operating Centre in Cardiff.

The West Midlands

Sectorisation did not always work as it should. On 21 April 1990, coal-sector-liveried Class 37 No. 37212 waits to leave Crewe with the 15:00 Manchester–Bristol parcels.

Crewe came into being as a railway station in 1837 with the opening of the Grand Junction Railway between Birmingham and Warrington. At that time Crewe was a hamlet of just 184 people on the estate of Lord Crewe, after whom the station was named. The Manchester to Birmingham railway opened between Manchester and Crewe in 1842. On 23 May 1992, No. 47095 passes through the station southbound with a train of BOC tanks.

At Silverdale Colliery, on 22 October 1992, Class 60 No. 60057 runs round its train. In later years the colliery had a production of 1 million tonnes per annum. It closed in 1998. The buildings and platform are of Silverdale station. The platforms remain but the buildings have been demolished.

The South Staffordshire Railway built a branch from Walsall to Cannock in 1859, in order to exploit the Cannock Chase coalfield. The Cannock Mineral Railway built the line from Cannock to Rugeley. Both were later absorbed by the LNW. The line lost its passenger service in 1965 but this was progressively restored between 1989 and 1998. The line has now been electrified. On 22 July 1994, No. 60073 Cairn Gorm approaches Brereton Sidings signal box with 6T58, the Rugeley Power Station to Essington Wood Opencast. This is now the site of Rugeley Town station.

The line between Lichfield and Anglesea Sidings is a remnant of the SSR, which remains open as a freight branch. Here we see No. 60068 *Charles Darwin* on 20 July 1995 approaching Fosse Way level crossing with the Brownhills Depot–Lindsey fuel oil empties.

Of the original sixteen stations between Shrewsbury and Hereford, now only Church Stretton, Craven Arms, Ludlow and Leominster remain open. Dorrington is the location of one of the closed stations. On 31 August 1991, No. 47201 passes with a mixed freight. The signal box dates from 1872. Notice the GWR lower quadrant signals, one of which has subsequently been replaced by a BR upper quadrant.

Class 31 No. 31530 *Sister Dora* is seen with an engineers' train in the Exchange Sidings at Wednesbury on 11 March 1993 This area is now the location of the Metro Centre depot and control room. No. 31530 went through a number of identities: starting out as D5695, then becoming successively Nos 31265 and 31430, and finally its present number. It has been preserved at Mangapps Railway Museum.

Ryecroft Junction was the meeting point of the Sutton Park line and the lines to Rugeley and Lichfield. On 18 April 1995, No. 31537 is seen arriving from the Sutton Park line with an engineers' train. The 31/5 class were 31/4 locomotives that had their ETH gear removed on transfer to the CE department.

Eastern England

Willington Power Station was situated between Stenson and North Staffordshire junctions on the Derby–Birmingham line. Opened in the late 1950s, it had a capacity to burn 8,000 tons of coal a day and, before the advent of MGRs, had 15 miles of track to handle the traditional wagons. On 21 September 1989, Class 20 Nos 20105 and 20047 are departing for Toton with empty MGR HAA wagons.

Pinxton is on the freight-only line that links Codnor Park Junction with Kirkby-in-Ashfield. The station of Pinxton and Selston opened with the railway in 1848 and closed ninety-nine years later. Pinxton signal box closed in 2007 after 110 years of service. It has been preserved at Barrow Hill. On 27 July 1991, Class 58 No. 58030, at the head of an empty MGR train, sets off after a signal check. Note that fixed to the Up starter signal (on the left) is a colour light signal. This was the Sleights East distant, which showed amber when the Pinxton home was pulled off and green when Sleights home was pulled off.

A busy scene at Welbeck Colliery Junction on 1 October 1992. Class 56 No. 56020 heads towards Shirebrook with a train of empties. Another Class 56 is in the process of running round its train on the branch. Once it departs, No. 58037, which is waiting at the signal, will draw forward and reverse on to the branch. Sadly, such scenes are but just a memory as all the collieries are now closed. The line remains in place and there have been discussions about reinstating a passenger service.

This is Elmton and Creswell Junction. Heading south on 13 March 1993 is Class 56 No. 56003 with an empty MGR train. The line behind the signal box once led to Bolsover and Barrow Hill. It has since been removed. The signal box is now permanently switched out. There is now a railway station at this location.

The branch from Little Eaton to Ripley opened in 1856. Passenger services ended in 1930 but the line remained open for freight traffic. On 7 July 1993, No. 56018 passes over Little Eaton level crossing with a train of coal from the Denby disposal point. Freight traffic ceased in 1999 and the track was lifted in 2012.

Class 56 No. 56020 approaches Worksop station with an eastbound MGR. The subsidiary signals seen on the left are for the Down reception sidings. These signals are no more, as both manual signal boxes at Worksop have been replaced by the new Worksop power signal box. The date is 20 April 1991.

With Chesterfield's distinctive church spire in the background Class 37s Nos 37250/37240 head south with steel coils from Lackenby on 10 May 1989.

In 1906 the North Lindsey Light Railway built a line from Frodingham to West Halton, later extended to Whitton. Dragonby sidings are situated on the Flixborough branch, which leaves the NLLR at Normanby Park. On 28 June 1993, RFS Industries No. 1 *Terence* shunts a train of steel bar.

Langham Junction. There is no junction as such here, but it is the beginning of a four-track section that reaches to Oakham. The subsidiary signal controls access to the Up Goods line. On 20 June 1991, No. 47332 heads south with a train of ballast.

The Lynn & Dereham Railway, which opened in 1848, closed in 1968 with the exception of the section to Middleton Towers, which was retained in order to service the sand quarries at that location. On 12 April 1995, Class 58 No. 58040 Cottam Power Station runs its train under the sand hopper at Middleton Towers station.

This is the site of Royston station. Returning from the Monk Bretton works on 31 March 1994 is Class 58 No. 58026 with empty wagons bound for Middleton Towers. This line has now been reduced to a single track.

On 20 June 1991, Class 47 No. 47332 approaches Gosberton crossing with a short engineer's train. The crossing was some distance away from the signal box, which can be seen in the background and had to be manned with its own cabin. Gosberton station closed in 1961, and since this photograph was taken the signal box has been closed and demolished and the crossing converted to automatic barriers.

Class 56 No. 56101 is seen on 12 April 1995 at Waldersea level crossing on the Wisbech–March line. The train is 6S93, the Wisbech–Deanside Nestle Purina pet food train. Passenger services were withdrawn in 1968 and the last freight train ran in 2000. Track remains in place and a number of plans to reopen the line have been put forward, but none has got much further than the discussion stage. It is reported that Network Rail have quoted a sum of £100 million to bring the line back to passenger status.

The magnificent array of signals at Wrawby Junction. The three gantries are for the Down Goods, the Down Slow and the Down Fast. The left-hand signal of each is for the Lincoln line, the centre for the Gainsborough line and the right-hand one is for the Scunthorpe line. On 5 September 1989, Class 37 No. 37075 is seen with a short train of tanks on the Down Fast line. The signal is pulled off for the Scunthorpe line. This engine has been preserved and is to be found at the Keighley & Worth Valley Railway.

At Ely on 13 September 1989 this view south from the station shows a Class 47 waiting with a train of tanks while alongside is Class 31 'Skinhead' No. 31450 with a postal train. This view has changed radically. The sidings on the right have been removed and the layout considerably modified. As well as this the route has been electrified and resignalled.

On 18 April 1990, Class 31s Nos 31327 and 31306 pull away from March Down Yard with a Freightliner service. The grey livery adopted by Railfreight when it became a separate entity in 1982 was improved by the addition of the red stripe in the mid-1980s, as worn by the leading engine.

London and the South

Reading was a crossroads for parcels and mail traffic during the 1980s. From late evening until the early hours, trains would arrive from destinations as far afield as Southend, Northampton, Liverpool, Bournemouth and Gillingham to be split up and reformed. On 5 February 1988, Class 33/1 No. 33108 waits to leave Reading with the 22:57 to Bournemouth, while Class 31 No. 31455 waits in the middle road.

Didcot A was a coal-fired power station and opened in 1968. It was located beside the main lines to South Wales and the Midlands so that it could be served with coal from either area. For most of its life it was provided with coal from the Nottingham Coalfield as this could enter and leave without reversing. With a capacity to burn 18,000 tons a day, there was normally a train every hour during the daytime. By the mid-1980s Class 58s were handling most of the traffic with occasional Class 56s. On 4 March 1988, Class 58 No. 58022 has discharged its load and heads past one of the cooling towers towards Foxhall Junction and the Oxford line

Before sectorisation took hold the parcels traffic at Reading produced a wide range of locomotive types. On 11 March 1988, Class 73/1 No. 73133 had arrived on the 20:00 from Basingstoke. In company with Class 33/2 No. 33206, it then took over the 17:22 Liverpool–Dover. This train had recently stopped operating with a TPO vehicle.

The Foster Yeoman Class 59s were primarily employed on the heavy 'Jumbo' trains between Merehead and Acton Yard that could load up to 4,000 tons. They were also used on some of the lighter turns. On 6 May 1988, No. 59003 is seen heading through the Wylie Valley, between Westbury and Salisbury, with the 07:17 Merehead–Botley formed of Yeoman PGA hoppers. These were a derivative of the HAA MGR hoppers.

Although the Southern Region lines west of Salisbury had been transferred to the Western Region in 1963, Meldon Quarry (near Okehampton) continued to provide ballast for the Southern Region. By the late 1980s this accounted for four trainloads a day hauled by pairs of Class 33s. Nos 33056 and 33002 are seen heading west at Heytesbury between Salisbury and Westbury on 11 May 1988.

Class 47 No. 47188 approaches Sherington with the 14:20 Westbury–Eastleigh Speedlink trip on 11 May 1988. Most of the vehicles are short wheelbase VEAs. These were converted from some of the later vacuum-braked Vanfits/Vanwides and equipped with air brakes and enhanced suspension to allow them to operate at 75 mph on Speedlink services. They were mainly used for MoD traffic in depots that would not accommodate the longer wheelbase wagons.

A regular turn for a Class 33 to Birmingham in 1988 was the 12:38 Gillingham–Preston mail train. The locomotive would then return south on the 17:22 Liverpool–Dover mail. On 27 July 1988, No. 33016 is seen heading north at Culham just south of Oxford.

On 23 September 1988, Class 47 No. 47357 is seen passing Cholsey with the return of the last regular flow of HTVs on the GW Main Line – blended coal from Newport Docks to Chinnor Cement Works. Travelling via Greenford and High Wycombe, it was by then the longest remaining flow for vacuum-braked coal wagons. They continued to be used until the last train to Chinnor on 20 December 1989.

The Esso refinery at Fawley processed a range of oil- and gas-related products that were carried by rail. On a frosty 17 December 1988, Class 47 No. 47198 has just passed Southampton station with empty LPG tanks.

A feature of the late 1980s was the variety of liveries being carried reflecting BR corporate, Railfreight and sectorisation. On 27 January 1989, Class 37s No. 37104 in Railfreight General livery and No. 37038 in corporate blue pass through Stratford with an eastbound container train.

Class 47 No. 47008 heads away from Ripple Lane with the 15:06 to Southampton MCT on 11 February 1989. Although the major depot at Stratford was only 3 miles away, Ripple Lane had a locomotive depot for traffic from the Dagenham and Barking areas.

By 1989 the North London line had been electrified overhead at 25 Kv AC, enabling electric locomotives to connect through from the West Coast to Stratford and East Anglia. On 3 March 1989, Class 85 No. 85012 heads north through South Kenton with the 12:45 Dagenham–Garston.

The 16:47 Eastleigh–Gloucester Speedlink was normally a Class 47, but on 18 August 1989 Class 37 No. 37104 was the booked locomotive. With a heavy train, Class 33 No. 33016 has been provided to assist and the pair make an unusual combination as they pass Sherrington at the head of the Wylie Valley.

From 1989 BREL (British Rail Engineering Ltd) refurbished London Underground stock at Crewe and Derby works. The refurbished stock ran south to Didcot overnight and was then tripped up to West Ruislip on Sunday mornings. Eight VDA wagons had the buffers lowered at one end and were recoded 'REA' for use as barrier wagons. On 18 March 1990, Class 31 No. 31296 is between Maidenhead and Reading returning from West Ruislip with stock for refurbishment.

On 2 August 1990, Class 56 No. 56043 passes Southampton with the 09:55 Ardingley–Whatley Quarry composed of ARC-owned JHA wagons. The locomotive bears the Construction sector livery of two-tone grey with blue and yellow square decals.

By 1990 Speedlink was struggling to survive financially. It was reported that the bulk flows between the major hubs only accounted for 15 per cent of the cost and the remainder on shunting and trip workings to final destinations. On 2 August 1990, Class 47 No. 47370 approaches Southampton with the 13:46 Salisbury–Eastleigh trip made up of clay slurry tankers from Quidhampton and MOD traffic from Chilmark.

Southampton boasted two container terminals. The MCT (Maritime Container Terminal) was in the Western Docks handling seaborne traffic, while the adjacent Millbrook terminal handled domestic containers and some Speedlink traffic. On 3 May 1990, Class 47 No. 47335 arrived with the 09:36 Ripple Lane–MCT. It is then seen arriving at Millbrook with wagons from the MCT and, after reversing in to collect more wagons, will form the 14:42 Millbrook–Willesden.

Impressed by the Foster Yeoman Class 59s, BR decided to build a third class of Type 5 locomotive with similar characteristics. The Class 60 had impressive performance ability, particularly with heavy trains. The Gulf War in 1990/1991 created an upsurge in MOD traffic and No. 60011, carrying Construction sector livery, is seen entering Sonning Cutting with a train of VDAs carrying MOD supplies.

Amey Roadstone Construction were impressed with Foster Yeoman's Class 59s and they ordered four of their own for their Whatley Quarry operations. Nos 59101–04 were delivered in 1990. On 11 April 1991, No. 59103 is seen between Reading and Maidenhead with a loaded train.

Running via Didcot and Reading the Rufford Colliery–Westbury Cement Works coal train bought a Toton Class 56 and HAA wagons onto the Berks & Hants line. On 13 April 1991, Class 56 No. 56019 appears to be in trouble with the 10:30 Westbury–Toton empties. It is seen passing Lower Basildon between Reading and Didcot with Dutch-liveried Class 47 No. 47315 doing all of the work.

By the early 1990s the Class 47s were nearing thirty years old, and pairs of Class 37s took over many of the container workings from Southampton. On 28 July 1992, Nos 37101 and 37074 head through Eastleigh with the 07:05 Coatbridge–Southampton MCT.

The South West

The line through Avonmouth to Severn Beach was the result of the efforts of three different companies: the GWR, the Midland and the Bristol Port Railway and Pier Company. In June 1995, Class 47 No. 47316 heads north through Hallen Marsh Junction with a train of car transporters.

By 1987 passenger work for Class 50s was in decline and consideration was given to using them on freight services. No. 50049 was equipped with modified Class 37 bogies, regeared for 75 mph, renumbered No. 50149 and repainted in Railfreight General livery. It was trialled on both Westbury stone and Cornish clay traffic. The project was not seen as a great success, due in part to the electronic anti-wheelslip mechanism having been removed during a mid-life overhaul at Doncaster. It spent most of its time at St Blazey covering for 37s being repaired from accident damage. On 8 April 1988 it has just passed Exminster with its regular turn, the 14:52 St Blazey–Gloucester. In 1989 it was rebogied for 100 mph, repainted and allocated to the Network South East pool.

Following the closure of Severn Tunnel Junction revised arrangements were made for Speedlink traffic, which was previously sorted there. On 31 May 1988, Class 47 No. 47258 passes Rewe with the 15:35 St Blazey–Gloucester, although most of the traffic would go on to Bescot for sorting. This locomotive had taken over at Exeter Riverside. The pair of Class 37/6s that had worked up from Cornwall then followed with the 20:15 Exeter Riverside–Westbury conveying cement and automotive traffic.

Following the closure of Stoneycombe Quarry (near Newton Abbot), Meldon Quarry supplied ballast to lines in the South West. Class 31 No. 31317 in Railfreight grey livery is passing Rewe, east of Exeter, with the 13:35 Meldon Quarry–Bristol East Depot on 31 May 1988.

From 1970 to May 1988 the 06:35 Bristol–Plymouth consisted of four passenger coaches and a handful of parcel vans providing a useful, if leisurely, service. With sectorisation, passenger and parcels services were separated and a DMU introduced. On 4 June 1988, Class 47 No. 47546 is a long way from its home depot of Inverness as it approaches Exeter St Davids.

A new flow introduced in 1989 was china clay slurry from Cornwall to Irvine in Scotland for the paper-making industry. The stainless-steel tanks were worked throughout by a pair of St Blazey Class 37s. On 11 April 1990, Nos 37673 and 37674 approach Langstone Rock with the 09:38 Burngullow–Irvine.

By 1990 a number of Laira's Class 50s were assigned to engineers' trains. On 31 May 1990, No. 50008 approaches Aller Junction with the 18:10 Exeter Riverside–Tavistock Junction.

On 7 April 1991, Class 47 No. 47096 was only three months away from withdrawal when it was assigned to work the 10:30 Exeter Central–Yeovil Junction ballast. It is seen arriving at Exeter Central having climbed the 1 in 33 incline from Exeter St Davids with the second portion of its load. The first portion had been bought up the previous day and is waiting in the goods yard.

By the late 1980s the vacuum-braked UCV 'clay hoods', used for carrying china clay, were life expired. A replacement was found by using redundant HAA wagons fitted with covers. On a dull summer's day in 1992, Class 37 No. 37669 is seen arriving at Lostwithiel with a loaded train for Fowey Docks.

Castleman's Corkscrew took an inland route through Dorset via Ringwood and Wimborne, thus avoiding the coastal town of Bournemouth. This was not thought to be a problem as, at that time, Bournemouth was little more than a hamlet. Bournemouth was finally reached by railway in 1870 when the LSWR opened a branch from Ringwood. Four years later the Poole and Bournemouth Railway approached the town from the opposite direction, completing its line to Bournemouth West on 15 June 1874. Branksome was on this stretch of line, but the station itself did not open until 1893. On 23 April 1992, No. 37803 heads through the station with the Cardiff Tidal to Hamworthy steel train.

Towards Privatisation

Prior to privatisation the government created three separate freight companies. These were Loadhaul, based in the North East; Transrail, based in the West; and Mainline, covering the South and East. At first these companies carried decals before some locomotives were painted in a new full livery. Only Loadhaul and Mainline did this; Transrail only ever used decals. In 1996 Loadhaul Class 60 No. 60064 is seen on the Grassington branch with a Hull–Rylstone empties working.

The line from Wrexham to Chester came into being as part of the North Wales Mineral Railway and was opened in November 1846. There were stations at Saltney, Rossett, Gresford and Wrexham. These were joined by Balderton in 1901 and later by the halt of Rhosrobin. Decline set in during the 1960s and all the intermediate stations were closed. In 1995, Transrail Class 56 No. 56018 is seen near Gresford with an Elgin–Dee Marsh service.

Class 37 No. 37672, wearing Transrail livery, is seen on the Sutton Oak branch with a short train approaching Hays Chemicals. This line is the remaining stub of the once busy line to Widnes. It closed progressively from 1951, just leaving the stub to Sutton Oak.

The Stenson Junction to Sheet Stores Junction line closed to passengers as early as 1930 but it remains an important freight route. On 7 July 1995, Class 58 No. 58012, with Mainline decals, heads west with a train of MGR empties.

Having delivered its load to Fiddlers Ferry Power Station, seen in the background, Mainline engine No. 60094 heads towards Warrington on the Widnes–Warrington freight-only line. The power station is due to close in 2020.